Contents

33

6

25

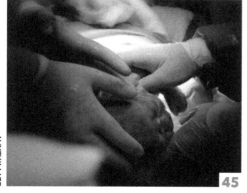

45

● All transcriptions by Eliza Frost

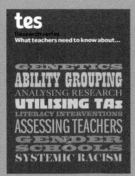

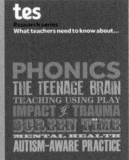

improve your teaching practice by keeping up to date with the latest education research from leading academics

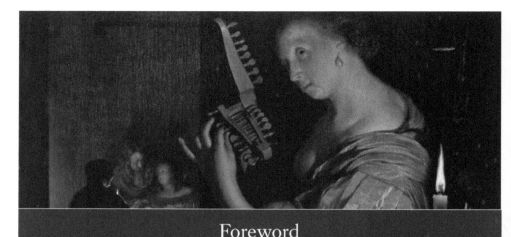

A little fine-tuning can help make the learning more harmonious

Learning is hard. Anyone who says otherwise is a liar. And if you have doubts about that statement yourself, this collection of interviews should put your mind at rest: they illustrate just some of the many elements a teacher has to weigh up on any given day, for any given child.

How is peer influence interacting with pupil wellbeing, and what impact could that be having on their behaviour or their ability to progress in comprehension? And how can you utilise Geary's work on primary and secondary knowledge to ensure that the early promise of children's numeracy progression lasts the pace?

Just considering these factors seems impossible, but the true scale of the interactions affecting learning is mind blowing.

Necessarily, teachers will make a lot of decisions intuitively: things in the classroom move so fast that it would be impossible for them to work otherwise.

Thus, with experience, teachers are able to conduct this enormous ragtag orchestra of variables with deft and expert skill.

But our hope for the *Tes* Podagogy podcast series, from which the following interviews are taken, is to try to make life in the classroom a little easier. We believe that by getting researchers to talk directly to teachers about their work, individual "variables" in that great ensemble of learning can be fine-tuned to make the process as effective and efficient as possible.

So while what follows can't remove the complexity of teaching completely, we hope that it can assist in cleaning up the white noise to make your life easier.

Jon Severs, Tes commissioning editor

Chapter 1
Professor David Geary
Are teachers being led astray by child-led learning?

How much of the knowledge required for a successful life can a child learn organically, without intervention?

This is the question posed by David C Geary, curators' professor in the department of psychological sciences at the University of Missouri. He developed a theory that states that children will be able to learn certain things – grouped under what he calls "primary knowledge" – through play, exploration and social interaction. But he also says that many other bits of essential knowledge – which he dubs "secondary knowledge"

– can be acquired only through direct teaching.

So, what does this mean for teaching practice? Here, he explains all.

Could you start by talking us through your definition of 'primary knowledge'?

Sure. By "primary", I mean human universal abilities. These are things that would go typically under the rubric of what's called folk psychology, folk biology and folk physics.

Folk psychology would include language, theory of mind, your ability to know what other people are thinking, reading facial expressions, body language and so forth.

Folk biology includes knowledge about plants and animals, which isn't that important for people in developed nations. But if you're living in the real world, you need an extensive knowledge base to survive.

And folk physics involves things like being able to navigate to get from one place to the other, knowing how to use tools, and so on.

These are competencies we see emerging in young children throughout the world. There's evidence for an implicit understanding of a number of these things, even in infancy, and it gets increasingly sophisticated during the course of development. This is the basic taxonomy of primary skills.

Do you mean the brain is 'primed' to learn these things?

Yes. The brain has a certain organisation to it, in certain areas, that makes sure that infants and young children find some things more interesting than others – human faces, for example. And then, by attending to human faces, that provides the experience that teaches them to recognise one person versus another, or discriminate a happy face from a sad face from an angry face.

So you have these built-in, early skeletal structures that guide kids' experience to make sure they get the feedback necessary to fill out these primary skills and adapt them to whatever their local conditions are.

What are secondary abilities?

By secondary, what I mean is evolutionarily novel knowledge. These are abilities, competencies, whatever you want to call it, that have emerged fairly recently in human historical time, maybe in the last few thousand years or so.

And it would include your typical academic skills studied in school: reading, writing, arithmetic. You don't need any of these competencies to survive and do well in traditional societies, but you certainly do need them today in developed societies.

So, in simplistic terms, they are a skill set that isn't a natural fit with how we are wired?

I don't think that's simplistic at all. That's exactly right: kids are biased towards, and tend to be interested in and easily learn about, certain types of things.

Kids all over the world do the same thing. But when you come to something like reading, for instance, it only emerges in cultures where there are institutions set up to teach kids how to read. It doesn't emerge in the same way that, say, language emerges.

Basic language comprehension, making inferences about the nuances of what somebody says and so forth – as long as it's an uttered sentence, that would all be part of the primary language base. Reading and writing skills are built on top of this, as well as some other systems, so there will be some overlap between the two.

In your papers, you discuss how this primary knowledge is essentially a natural acquisition of knowledge.

Right. There's a built-in inherent structure that gets you started. You focus on that, you begin to make inferences, but then, through exploring the ecology, exploring the environment, playing with animals or hunting them or whatever, you begin to learn more about the specifics of the plants and animals in their particular region.

Another example: you could put a kid in any natural language community and, by talking to the kid and them socially engaging with other people, that language will become the language that they're exposed to. But the underlying structure is the same for all people.

So, if primary knowledge develops in 'free' exploration, what should we be doing when children enter the structured environments of early years education? Would a more formal EYFS disrupt the process?

I don't think anybody knows for sure what the sufficient amount of unstructured time is to make sure primary knowledge develops. It's probably not huge. Kids can play during breaktime, unstructured. They could play after school with their friends, presumably they'll have weekends to play. That's probably sufficient.

Is there any evidence that a lack of exploration time can be detrimental?

There are some interesting studies in folk biology looking at your understanding of the relations between different species.

And if you take a 10-year-old living in a traditional context, they have really well-developed folk biological knowledge, because they've had a huge amount of experience interacting with the natural world. You take 10-year-olds from an urban area in a developed nation – they still have the basic structure of folk biology but it's not very rich. They don't have the depth of detail because they're not having many experiences with the natural world.

That's not necessarily an issue because they're not going to have to go out and find food on their own. But it does show that if kids don't get enough experiences in these areas, they're not going to become as sophisticated as they otherwise would.

Would spatial abilities, so crucial for maths, be considered primary knowledge?

Yeah, the question on spatial abilities is a great one. That would be a part of folk physics. There are different types of spatial abilities. Basically, knowing where you are, where you need to be and how to get back – those sorts of things. These skills develop during childhood and probably into adolescence, and there is some evidence that restricted exploration of the large-scale environment does or can affect these skills.

So, is your argument that primary knowledge largely does not need a teacher's intervention?

With the primary learning, kids can kind of hum along, do what they're going to do, play, explore things, figure out how things work, etc – all child-generated activities, and they don't have to put much effort into it because, as I said, the brain is pre-prepared to take those experiences and flesh out these primary skills. There's not much in terms of needing a lot of effort there.

But once you get to the non-evolved skills – reading, writing and so forth – the brain isn't structured to easily learn those. The instructional environment has to provide that organisation to the child's experiences.

So, does the teaching have to have a relationship with the primary models in the brain, or is it that the teacher is providing the structure that the brain is not providing? How does that interaction work?

I'm seeing it as that the teacher is providing the structure that the brain is not providing. I think one of the primary or important points of the distinction between primary and secondary is that the things that are sufficient for learning in primary domains (language, spatial navigation, etc) are not going to be sufficient for learning in secondary domains. And there have been educational theories that have not made that distinction and have given us things like whole language and whole maths.

The Montessori style of education? The self-discovery?

Yeah, that's self-discovery. But that's for preschoolers. And I don't think it's as big of a deal for preschoolers, except the ones who have some issues at home. They're not getting enough exposure to letters and numbers. Once you get to real academic learning, the child discovering things just isn't going to work.

Is there any consensus in the literature around when we shift from this primary child-

exploration type of knowledge acquisition to this secondary academic acquisition?

I think the primary acquisition is always going on. You're always learning more about people and relationships, for example. Even into adulthood, you get more sophisticated, more knowledgeable, hopefully wiser, so that continues.

Since the secondary acquisitions are evolutionarily novel, I don't think we can think of them in terms of the developmental readiness. There are what's called life history stages in biological development but this is outside of that process.

We do know, from studies conducted here in the US, and I'm sure elsewhere, that there are certain things that kids really need to know to be ready for formal academic learning – whenever that happens. So, recognising letters, recognising numerals, maybe having a bit of phonemic awareness, understanding numbers conceptually. Kids who are delayed in that, for whatever reason, start out at a disadvantage whenever they start school. And it's very difficult for them to catch up.

You've spoken before about the fact that the primary knowledge can get in the way of the secondary knowledge?

There have been some pretty good studies on that in folk biology and folk physics. People have "folk ideas" – meaning general intuitive ideas about things like motion, things like biological growth or evolution – that provide good enough explanations for day-to-day sorts of things but are scientifically incorrect.

The interesting thing is, you can teach people the science and they get it. And even if they're, say, an undergraduate in biology, their intuitive folk ideas about growth in evolution remain intact, like they have two systems of knowledge. If they're not careful, they could easily slip into the primary biases.

The intuitive stuff works pretty well, particularly in a traditional context. You don't really need to understand things scientifically. But if you're in a developed nation and you're expected to understand certain scientific concepts, then these intuitive biases can get away.

So, are we biased to our primary intuitive sense?

Yeah, we are definitely biased towards our primary intuitive sense of things because understanding something from a secondary or scientific perspective takes a lot of effort, unless you are super familiar with the information.

How much of this science can we translate to actual educational practice?

The translation happens, in part, through cognitive load theory. So, [in] part of my other writings on primary and secondary [knowledge], I argue that to construct secondary knowledge involves explicit attention-driven engagement of working memory and inhibition of any kind of folk biases – cognitive load theory offers a way for teachers to ensure that happens.

If kids are just fooling around playing with one another, doing stuff, they feel happy. A part of the brain called the default mode is probably very active. That gives them a sense of monitoring how things are going and puts their sense of self in a social context, which is great. For mind

Do you advocate any explicit way of doing that?

Well, that's where the art of teaching comes in. You really have to get the kids engaged in the material in some way.

There are kids who have difficulties maintaining attentional control or they have poor working memory skills – they really can't deal with a lot of information at a time. There are interventions in development that are looking to put in scaffolds to help kids with those types of deficits. They've only started to be done in the past few years for maths.

But I think there are things that teachers can do is grab attention for most kids. And then there are some kids where they're going to need additional scaffolding in their instruction, maybe giving smaller bits of information, having them repeat it and other strategies.

It's more pleasurable to be in the default mode, presumably?

It is absolutely more pleasurable to be in the default mode rather than the attentional focus and executive function working memory mode, because that takes effort. To sit there and focus on something you have to actively inhibit the default mode and think about what you're trying to learn. It not something that people easily do and it's not something they like to do.

That's why people jump to conclusions based on their intuitive sense of things, rather than stopping and thinking it through logically. Because if your intuitive sense of something seems good enough, you're going to go with it. Why go through all this effort of thinking it through?

This is an edited version of an interview that took place in February 2019. To hear the original podcast, go to bit.ly/Acquisitions_Geary

wandering, just daydreaming, that's the default mode network.

But if you need to learn, say, algebra, you need to really focus on the information. You need to focus on whatever the teacher is doing or whatever is in the book, because it's very abstract, not easy-to-learn information. That attentional focus kicks in a different brain region called the dorsal attentional network and that actually inhibits the default mode network and vice versa.

Once you switch on that attentional focus, and I guess that can be done through controlling the learning environment, I guess there are several ways to grab attention as a teacher: you can demand it or you can do something that attracts attention.

Chapter 2

Professor Jane Oakhill
We need a more comprehensive approach to comprehension

Reading is often taught as a process of decoding words, with understanding of the text coming second. This isn't the right approach, says Jane Oakhill, professor of experimental psychology at the University of Sussex and leading expert on the teaching of comprehension and inference. She believes schools need to adopt a more joined-up approach and teach all elements of reading together.

Many schools approach the teaching of literacy as a two-step process: decoding followed by comprehension. Is it really that simple?

No, I don't think it can be that simplistic. Schools should be teaching comprehension skills from the start. It shouldn't be "first, we do decoding and then we move on to comprehension". That is giving children the wrong idea about reading.

I think this is why some [children] go on to have comprehension problems, because they come to believe that reading is about decoding, about getting the words right. And actually, we know that better comprehenders believe that it's really about understanding the text, getting the meaning of the text.

That is combined with the fact that we're increasingly hearing that many children come to school with inadequate language skills, inadequate vocabulary. It's crucial that we focus on those language skills, the inference skills – really thinking deeply about texts right from the start.

There is evidence that even preschool children who have the ability to make inferences before they can read – from videos or from listening to stories – are the ones who turn out to be better comprehenders later on.

I have seen some fantastic comprehension work done with Reception class children, most of whom couldn't read a single word. The teacher had a picture book and was talking them through it, reading the text to them, discussing it with them, getting them to make predictions. That's what we need at preschool if possible but, certainly, from the first stage of schooling. Not one and then the other, but both in parallel.

So, do you think children need to be able to understand what they are reading, even in those early stages of decoding?

Children should be encouraged to know what's going on. Nowadays, even the books for beginning readers are made interesting for children, so there is some intrigue, perhaps some moral to the story, that they can extract. If they're just reading the words, they're going to miss that.

So, should you stop a child who is just learning to decode in the middle of reading to ask them what is happening in the story?

You shouldn't necessarily be constantly stopping the child who is struggling to read the words, but that could be done sometimes so that they do get the idea that they're supposed to be understanding as well as reading.

Something that I say to teachers a lot is that children don't have to be reading in order to learn to understand written text.

There is a huge amount that can be done with oral language and some of the best instruction in comprehension that I've seen has been in classrooms where the teacher has encouraged lots of targeted discussion addressing specific questions in groups, followed by feedback and further discussion in a plenary session. Talking is so important and I think that is something that is very often missed out.

Let's say you have a cohort of Reception children. How different will they be in their natural comprehension ability?

I don't know any data on that but I'm sure there are huge variations in those children, particularly in their language skills and vocabulary. I can't remember the precise numbers but there are some statistics on the average vocabulary of a child coming from a middle-class, literate home background, where they have been read to and the parents are avid readers, and the child coming from a less privileged background, where parents don't read much and don't read to the child. There is

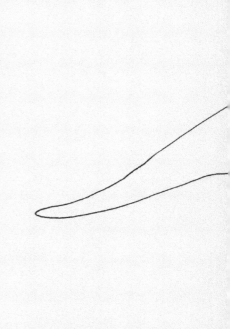

going to be huge variation in vocabulary and in language skills.

Shockingly, even in the UK, some children coming to school are not really capable of stringing a sentence together, whereas others are very competent. That obviously is going to feed into their comprehension skills. That's one of the reasons why I think it's so important to get started on language for comprehension as early as possible.

Almost all children are going to benefit, to some extent because you're giving them

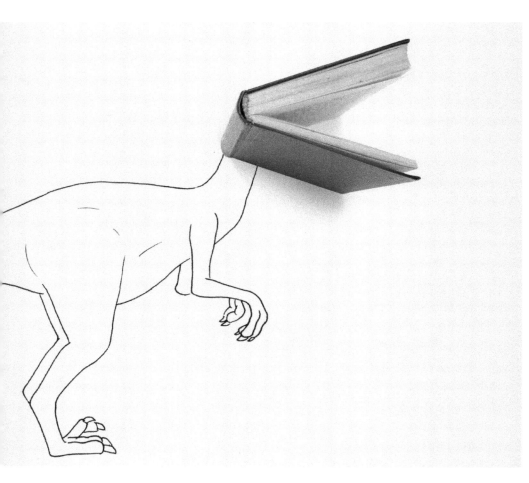

the tools, even the ones from the more privileged homes and backgrounds.

You're giving them tools to think about language and reading – those are metacognitive tools to help them think about their own understanding.

How early should we start the vocabulary-building process in schools? And what is that process of vocabulary building?

As early as possible, again, particularly with those children who really need it. We need to be telling them vocabulary and also helping them to work out word meanings because that's going to be increasingly important once they start to read.

Obviously, with preschool children and when children first start learning to talk, people are pointing things out for them and telling them what things are called, encouraging them to use new words.

But once children start reading, the evidence is that most of their vocabulary comes through reading, not through being explicitly taught words. In fact, the

meta-analyses of vocabulary instruction are not very promising. It's really quite hard to teach older children new vocabulary effectively. It is possible, but the transfer effects are not great and, in general, people agree that teaching vocabulary explicitly is not the way forward.

What we really need to do is help children to develop their own vocabulary. Again, these are metacognitive skills. Skilled readers don't necessarily go to a dictionary unless they keep seeing a word they don't know and it's disrupting their understanding. They might form an impression of what the word means from the context and refine their meaning, again from the context. If I'm still finding that it doesn't quite fit, I realise I haven't quite got the right meaning, so I have to adjust it a little bit.

This is what we need to be teaching children to do, not just to immediately ask or pull out the dictionary – though those might be useful strategies as well – but to try to work out what's going on, which is probably related to their inference skills. If they're good at using context to make inferences about text, then vocabulary learning could be regarded as a product of those inference skills.

So we're talking about exposure to vocabulary rather than explicit instruction?

Yes, exposure, but also teaching the children to think about what the word might mean in the context. For example, if the teacher knows that a child or children don't know the meaning of a word, rather than just telling them, it would be much more effective to have a discussion about what the word could mean in this context.

Perhaps with a small group, ask: "Does anybody have any ideas about what this word might mean? Why do you think that? Let's go back to the text. Would that meaning fit with the text? If not, why not?" – getting them to really think about word meaning in an active way, not in a passive "learning definitions" way.

Do some children just develop inference skills naturally? Or does it all stem from the richness of their home environment and experiences?

I don't know of any evidence that specifically addresses that. But I would certainly think that there is probably an element of both, as there often is. Children who are born with certain genes are likely to develop those skills or just have higher verbal ability. I think, too, that an environment where parents or caregivers are getting children to discuss and think about things, and argue about topics, is going to improve their thinking skills and their inference skills more generally.

How important is a knowledge-rich curriculum to developing comprehension abilities?

It's going to be impossible to teach children the huge bank of knowledge that they need to know to tackle texts that they might come across.

Clearly, knowledge is important in text comprehension. I hope I would have at least an adequate understanding of most texts in psychology. But if I tried to read a text in quantum mechanics, I would be absolutely floored. My general comprehension skills might be quite good, but because I don't have the background knowledge, I would be completely lost.

But if I really wanted to know a lot about quantum mechanics, the way I would tackle that is to find the "dummy's guide" to quantum mechanics or some much more elementary text to give me a lead into the basic concepts and vocabulary.

Going back to children in school, it's a really good idea for teachers to encourage children to activate background knowledge and use that in their understanding. Some children don't do that. I've heard cases where children say, "Oh, am I allowed to use what I know about the world to understand this text?" This has been a real "light-switch" moment for them. [Until then] they think that texts are self-contained somehow.

We need to encourage children to use what knowledge they've got, but what if they haven't got any knowledge of this topic?

Yes, obviously, if you give them the rudiments, then that could be helpful. But my problem with it is, how are we going to do that throughout the children's lives? What about when they leave school and

they want to learn something and there is not someone there who has got the knowledge base in a package for them? What are they going to do then?

As with vocabulary, we've got to get children actively engaged in learning, because most of the knowledge that they gain is not something that people are going to tell them in a preparatory way to read a text; it's knowledge that they're going to glean from the text.

Of course, those texts have to be at an appropriate level. Going back to the quantum mechanics, you've got to find a sufficiently introductory-level text to get them started.

My problem with knowledge and vocabulary is, where does this information come from? I think a lot of it has to come from the child themselves, using strategies to build that knowledge, to build that vocabulary. People are talking in a dichotomised way at the moment about

vocabulary, and knowledge and comprehension strategies. What we should be looking at is how these things can support each other.

Do you find that comprehension improves if a child is interested in what they are reading and is therefore more motivated to understand it?

I did a study a few years ago looking at boys' and girls' motivation to read and how that affected their comprehension. There was something in the press about the Year 6 Sats tests that year and people said they thought the boys' performance was better than usual because the texts were all about spiders. The assumption was that this would be intrinsically interesting and more motivating for boys.

So, the following year, we gave two texts to children who hadn't seen them. We gave them the spiders text and another text that was about children who were evacuated during the Second World War to live with other families. We just gave the children the titles at the start and asked them which they thought they would rather read. The vast majority of the boys said they would prefer to read the text about spiders and the vast majority of the girls said they would prefer to read the text about the children being evacuated.

We then got them to read both texts and asked them questions about both. What we found was that the girls did equally well whatever text we threw at them, so their comprehension level didn't change. But the boys did significantly better on the text about spiders than they did on the other text, which they weren't so motivated to read. I think gender is almost certainly not the only variable that affects children's

GETTY

motivation. I'm sure we could find effects in girls if we could find sufficiently motivating or demotivating texts.

So, I think children reading texts that they want to find out something from is really important in getting them motivated early on.

What else do we need besides a secure knowledge base and sufficient vocabulary to be able to comprehend a text well?

The skills that consistently seem to be important are inference abilities: both linking up information in the text and putting together ideas across the text as a whole, and relating that to relevant background knowledge. There has been a large meta-analysis published very recently showing that training in inference skills is effective in building comprehension.

Another area that I've touched on is meta-cognitive understanding. These are not entirely independent. Meta-cognitive understanding would be the ability to reflect on your own understanding.

It's about knowing when you don't get it but also knowing what to do if you don't get it. That might be because we have a lapse of attention, particularly if it's something that we don't particularly want to read but have to read. We realise that, actually, we haven't been taking in this text and we pretty much know where our attention lapsed and where we have to go back to in order to correct that lapse and make sure we have got the meaning of the last few lines, the last page, or whatever.

Another reason you might not 'get' it is that you need to make an inference – that something has happened in the text that doesn't quite connect up, so you need to actively think about how you might make it connect up.

Some inferences can be quite deliberate, but a lot of inference-making just happens automatically in skilled readers. We don't really realise that it's going on.

How early can we identify those children who will struggle with comprehension?

I think probably earlier than we are. With suitable tools, teachers could start identifying children as soon as they start school. Unlike with dyslexia or word decoding problems, with comprehension there aren't any standard early indicators of children who might have these difficulties.

Most of the children who have comprehension problems are perfectly good at holding everyday conversations; they're perfectly good communicators. It's the text language that they're not getting. They can have interactions with someone face to face because, of course, those are very different to understanding a body of text. You've got the contextual cues, the nodding of somebody who is understanding or the frowning if they're not.

Many of them are also good decoders. A general problem is that teachers very often don't identify children with comprehension problems because they're good at decoding. They're diligent children, which is probably why they've learned to decode, and they get on with their schoolwork.

It might not be until late primary school, when there's more pressure on reading to learn, that these children who are having difficulties become apparent. We need to try to identify them much earlier so that we can encourage and develop their comprehension skills from the start.

This is an edited version of an interview first published in June 2019. To listen to the original podcast, go to bit.ly/OakhillComp

Chapter 3
Dr Simon Edwards
Unteachable pupils?
There's no such thing

S imon Edwards is a senior lecturer in youth studies at the University of Portsmouth. Edwards has held positions across the education spectrum, from mainstream teacher to teaching in alternative provision. He is now a researcher working with children deemed too tough even for pupil referral units (PRUs).

Here, he explains why there is no such thing as an "unteachable" child.

Is there such a thing as an unteachable child?

No. There is no such thing as an unteachable child. But I think there's a series of coinciding events that sometimes occur within the classroom that lead to that child not being able to engage with the classroom learning.

For example, I was trying to teach algebra to a 14-year-old girl whose mum had suffered a stroke when the girl was 9. As a result, this girl was constantly worried about her parent being ill. This meant that while she was in school, she would always have her mobile phone on and wanted to know her mum was OK.

When the school became an academy, phones were not allowed and we had to put them in a cupboard and lock them in there. That, of course, became quite problematic for her if the phone went off or if it had been longer than an hour since she was able to check it.

That's an example showing that, sometimes, events coincide within the classroom where the young people cannot focus on the lesson at that moment. But they are not unteachable generally.

So schools deem children unteachable based on too strict a set of rules and criteria?

We know that some behaviour policies are designed in order to exclude some young people because you know that some young people are not going to be able to comply.

For example, I went to an alternative provision school where I spoke with the pupils for some research on non-attendance. They told me: "We get a behaviour point for not having a pencil in the morning, we get a behaviour point for having the wrong coloured shoes on, we get a behaviour point for not having the top button done up or a tie on. And if you get three behaviour points, you get half a day exclusion." How can we define not having a pencil as a behaviour?

There are these actions that are being turned into moral actions, and then laid on the student as a way of making them comply and somehow be a more efficient learner – but it's based on fear.

So there's no appreciation of a student's context or reality?

Yeah, you've got a youngster whose mum has got three part-time jobs because she's by herself, then this young person needs to get up in the morning, get their own breakfast and get to school on their own – the last thing they think is, "Oh, I need a pencil".

Do schools make enough effort to accommodate social reality or adapt behaviour policies?

I was doing some research in a school in the South East last year and was asked to look at low attainment by disadvantaged boys. We did 40 interviews with some of the students, right from Years 1 and 2 up to Year 10. We interviewed school leaders, some parents and the children. Then we did focus groups, then we did a literature review to put it in the wider context.

In the primary school, the emphasis was really looking at a wraparound service towards the young people. It didn't want to label the kids, so they didn't look for any disadvantage in a sense. And I completely get that, and the feel in that primary school was lovely and the kids were really happy.

But the problem with that is, by the time they then got to secondary school, which is much more GCSE focused, you've got no real data to go on that you can start to address so that you can then put interventions in place.

Consequentially, there was a difficulty in the transition – the challenge was not spotted or addressed early enough, or at all.

The arguments for exclusion usually revolve around safety. Do you think that is a factor in a child becoming 'unteachable'?

Certainly on safety, there are some young

people who have issues so severe and things going on at home, and they just can't survive and cope within a school classroom with 30 or 40 kids in there. I completely understand that.

And what about aspirations as a 'cure' for challenging behaviour – it's often claimed that higher aspirations mean children can be more on task?

I've had a couple of other headteachers, particularly in low-income areas, say we need to raise the pupils' aspirations, and I think: "What are you on about?"

Loads of the young people who I work with and talk with want to be like their dad who is a builder, or their mum who's a hairdresser or doing admin. So they have got aspirations. What you're saying is you want to raise their aspirations to the aspirations of those kids who are middle class or come from a more affluent background.

But if you have a child whose mum is a doctor or a dad who's a solicitor or a teacher or whatever, then their aspirations are no higher really – or they might actually have lower aspirations in terms of where their starting line is than another young person.

So don't tell me a child doesn't have high aspirations. In fact, I did some research in a school last year where I was looking at attainment – and the aspirations of the kids were through the roof.

When you speak to Years 1 and 2, you get a lot of "I want to be a footballer" because they live near the football stadium area. By the time you get to Year 10, you get "I want to be a footballer but I want to do it this way – I want to work for the local club, or I want to be a manager". It's much more realistic by that point.

You mentioned parents – do schools need to do more to get them on side as allies?

Absolutely. But it must be saying: "I'm not asking you to help me do my job and I'm not here to tell you how to do your job."

When I was in a special school, I used to say to the parents: "I'm here to serve you, and help you and your child get where you want to go in life."

Of course, sometimes the child doesn't know where they want to go, but we have to find a way in to talk to them to try to get them to find an alternative [path].

So we need to do whatever we can to foster a sense that school will benefit them, even if that's done subtly?

I worked with some youngsters who had an old Mini motor and we took it into the garden and stripped the engine apart.

Doing this enabled us to have a conversation about how to work out the circumference and volume of a cylinder barrel. This led to one lad saying he wanted to be a mechanic. I said: "Why don't you be an engineer, or a designer or an architect?" We were chatting about that while we were taking the motorcycle engine apart. And when he got home, he said: "Mum, I want to become an engineer."

His behaviour went up from -6 points to +20 [on our behaviour scale] within three weeks, just because of that conversation.

But this also brings back the point about parents because, at the same time, one of my team had been talking to the boy's mum. The mum didn't know what to do: she said he was a pain and that they kept fighting physically as well. One of my team is going: "Yeah, but you need to understand where he is coming from."

That sounds like mentoring in both cases.

The crux of what we were doing in our project was, we said to the parent and the boy: "You have the capability, but you don't have the resources."

If you haven't got the capability right now, we believe you have the ability to develop the capability to access the resources that you need.

Overall, is this an issue that's getting better or worse?

Well, too many children are getting excluded. And not always for the right reasons.

What advice would you give to schools on this?

When I ran my pupil referral unit, the pupils and I and my team wrote

the behaviour rules together. As unbelievable as it sounds, the kids ended up being stricter on themselves than the school was.

They're buying in, essentially?

Yeah, if you want to put it that way. They trust in me. That's the responsibility. They're saying: "Si, you're the educator, you've got a set of skills that we want and you're promising us that it will help us get a good life."

And I think positivity really counts. Last year, a headteacher asked me: "What do you think of the kids [at my school]?" I said: "They're lovely." And he said: "Really? I think they're the worst behaved kids I've ever come across in my life."

He had just excluded 65 young people and when I asked why, he said: "I've got to set the line."

I said: "OK, fine." But I added that my experience of living on housing estates and working with youngsters from the sort of background that his schools were in is that the parents will go: "Fine, we'll take the hit and we believe in the system and that what you're saying is going to work."

But I told the headteacher: "As soon as it doesn't work, as soon as the second or third time the kid has been excluded for not having the right coloured shoes on, or not having the top button done up or because he's answered back, or because he's asked too many questions of a teacher and raised his voice – as soon as Mum has to come out of her job and she's on hourly pay so she loses an hour or two of pay to help her kid – all you're going to do is build up resentment if you don't also address the problem in the classroom.

"Because the punishment has not worked, has it? The behaviour is continuing. And, effectively, you're placing all the blame on the child and the family and things other than what you're doing in the classroom."

I tell schools: "If your pedagogy, the way you teach, could be adjusted or changed, or you could work with your young people in a different way or vary the curriculum so it's more appropriate, then that would create a more inclusive environment and the kids might be more motivated and go in."

You need to work with young people and listen to their voice and help them to be part of the process.

This is an edited version of an interview that took place in July 2019. To hear the original podcast, go to bit.ly/Exclude_Edwards

GETTY

Chapter 4
Professor Daniel Ansari
**What really counts in
early maths teaching?**

ALAMY

Daniel Ansari is a professor in the department of psychology at the University of Western Ontario in London, Canada, where he heads the Numerical Cognition Laboratory. He has concentrated his efforts on trying to unpick one specific area of maths: the origins of number and how we teach children to count. He explains how a child's development is not linear nor universal, and why we have "to be very careful about putting children into certain categories at an early age".

Is the act of counting equivalent to the act of reading, in the sense that it is not a natural activity but one that we've created, as humans, to get on?

That's a really interesting question and one that researchers in the field of numerical cognition have been grappling with. There is no doubt that we share with other species a sense of quantity and some people have referred to that as an "approximate magnitude system", meaning that we can judge "more" or "less".

Animals can have a rough representation of the number of items they're presented with. It is our exact numerical abilities that are uniquely human. For example, the count sequence is, I think, the first foray that children make into a precise representation of number.

If we look around the world, we know from the studies of anthropologists that there are populations that have count words only for quantities up to three – beyond that they say "many" or "more". They use quantifiers.

The count sequence does seem to be a uniquely human thing that has developed over the course of cultural history.

Then, of course, the verbal count sequence gets a link to the visual representation of numerical symbols, such as Hindu or Arabic numerals, that are almost a universal visual symbolic representation of number across the world now. In other words, there does seem to be some rudimentary sense of quantity that we're born with, that we share with other species, for which we can also study the

numbers, such as 1,432, requires a lot of different processes, it requires quite a good understanding of place value, it involves an understanding of symbolic number.

But we don't really know when people are processing such large numbers whether they are imagining a quantity that is associated with that or not.

It is different from processing words, but there isn't a lot of research to suggest that number words are processed differently from written Hindu or Arabic numerals or multi-digit number sequences.

You mentioned anthropological studies and the fact that people understand quantity. Is there an innate sense – say, if we're building a structure – of trigonometry, for example?

That is a hotly debated topic in the field. Some people argue that we are born with an approximate sense of number, so that just as we can perceive colours, we can perceive numbers. There is also other research to suggest that maybe it's not numerical quantity that we are born to process but it's all sorts of quantity. It's length, height, density, area. Out of this more generalised magnitude system, we build a precise numerical system.

At this point, we're still trying to figure out exactly what are the origins of our numerical abilities, and there's some substantial controversy in the field around that and a lot of active research.

There has been a lot of talk about spatial ability and the link to number. Could you explain more?

There's certainly a lot of research to show that numerical and spatial abilities are closely intertwined in the brain over

brain mechanisms, but it is only humans that have a precise, infinite count sequence to exactly represent the number of items in the set.

When we read a number or sequence of numbers, such as 1,432, do our brains process it in the same way as a word?

We understand that processing large

the course of development. There's a lot of exciting new work examining how one can strengthen spatial abilities and how that might transfer to maths learning and to the acquisition of numerical skills.

When it comes to the brain, the areas involved in number processing are also involved in spatial processing. One of the things we think is that spatial visualisation might be incredibly important for maths. In a way, you're using your visual spatial working memory and your spatial representation to form a mental workspace within which you can represent numerical and mathematical relations. That might be one way of thinking about the relationship between space and number.

It's exciting because more and more preschools, at least here in Canada, are focusing on developing students' spatial thinking – and that might give them a really important scaffold for geometry and more complex numerical spatial relationships, and processing those later on.

You've spoken before about trying to create an equivalent journey for maths learning to the journey for literacy. Is that still a focus?

I first started thinking about that when I was doing my PhD at UCL back in the early 2000s and the question came up: what are some of the key components that need to be in place for kids to even learn this skill of numeracy?

That's where the analogy to phonological awareness became apparent to me. There were some publications on this around that time and this was when the field of numerical cognition was growing, too, and people were really hopeful that we could discover this basic underlying number sense.

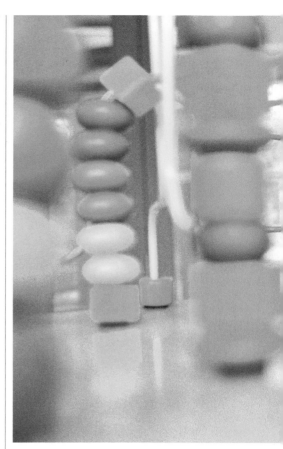

It quickly became apparent that it probably isn't as straightforward as it is in reading because in maths there are so many things. As my maths educator friends would remind me, number is only one of the many things that makes up the domain of maths.

I then decided when I opened my own research laboratory that I would focus specifically on the origins of number.

Where we're going now is more and more towards understanding how children learn numerical symbols, how that provides an important scaffold and how learning numerical symbols is a really complex thing.

So, we're trying to tackle all these different ways of processing numerical symbols as a means to better understand which of these processing aspects is most important for maths learning and also using that to inform screening to potentially identify children who might be at risk of developing mathematical difficulties.

Is there even a linear path where certain steps are learned first, then second and so on?

Development is not linear, it's not neat, it's not universal across all children.

When it comes to the development of counting and the understanding of the meaning of counting – what some people refer to as the cardinality principle – we have quite good evidence that, in most children, the ability to recite the count sequence comes before their understanding of the meaning of the count sequence.

That tends to be a very gradual process whereby children first become "1 knowers", so they know that "1" refers to one item. Then they become "2 knowers", and "3 knowers" and

"4 knowers". Eventually they become what we refer to as "cardinality principle knowers".

That transition from a procedural ability to count but not really understanding what that means to having an understanding is one of the most fundamental steps in early numeracy development. Children make it roughly between the ages of two and a half up to about 5, because there's a huge amount of variability in when they make that leap from being able to recite the count sequence to understanding what the purpose of counting is.

Does it matter at which point a visual representation of the number is introduced?

The most important thing early on when it comes to the development of number is, in my view and from what we know from research, first developing an understanding of the verbal number sequence and then introducing the written number sequels after that. At that point, it really is very much a process of transcoding because you have already developed a representation of cardinality for the spoken number words and now you're just mapping that on to the written symbols.

So, should we be careful about judging mathematical ability based on what a child can write down or read rather than what they can recite?

That's an interesting idea. Certainly, we shouldn't think too narrowly about ways of getting an idea of what children know about maths, number and numerical relations early in primary school. And there should still be use of manipulatives to assess children's understanding and for teachers to get an insight into how they're thinking about quantity.

It's important because, as with reading, children come into the early years with huge variability in their knowledge, huge variability in their skills, and we need to give children who may not have had the opportunity in their homes to learn Arabic numerals an opportunity to show what else they might know about quantities so that teachers can scaffold them adequately.

So what is the optimal teaching approach in EYFS – should we be sitting children down and telling them things formally, or letting them play and discover?

That's still very much a topic of debate and people are trying to run good empirical studies to compare approaches.

When it comes to play-based [learning], I think one of the common misunderstandings is that it implies a purely constructivist approach to education, one in which children discover concepts through play.

But I think some of the most effective play-based work is when teachers are using it as an opportunity to carry out direct instruction – to direct children's attention, for example, to numerical relations.

Just free play is probably unlikely to lead to great leaps in the kinds of conceptional development that we might want from children in the early years in order to prepare them for what comes next. But a combination of play and intentional instruction can be very effective.

It's also extremely challenging for educators. I see that a lot here in Ontario. The school boards are doing a lot of work with their teachers and early childhood

educators to get them to think about how they can be participants in play in a way that allows them to direct children's attention to important concepts. Play-based learning is very attractive; it's also very challenging.

Certainly, a play-based approach can be more engaging for children and maybe more age appropriate, but I do think it needs to be intentional. It can't just be, "here is a set of blocks, now go away and play with it and we expect you to develop a concept of number".

How do we guard against a purely procedural understanding of number?

Procedural versus conceptual understanding – or skills versus comprehension – is a debate very much alive in the maths world. I don't think there is a simple answer to this. What research from psychology and the science of learning have shown is that it's very hard to separate procedural skills from conceptual understanding and that they're iteratively related.

Do you think that we are close to being able to pinpoint key areas of the numeracy journey and therefore unpick the challenges children have, in the same way that we can with reading?

I certainly think that we are further away than developmental language difficulties or developmental dyslexia, simply because the empirical work has a much longer history than in the domain of maths. But we are making progress towards identifying some of the key building blocks of certain aspects of maths that we can screen for earlier on.

I'm thinking about some of the work that we and some others have done around being able to recognise numerals, being able to judge which of two numerals is larger, and we're seeing some fairly good evidence that is predictive of later maths skills and that these kinds of measures can discriminate between children with and without maths difficulties.

But just as is the case for dyslexia, I think one needs to be aware that if one screens early on, you may have a child in front of you who looks like they might need an intervention but, because of the non-linearities of development and how things change, that child six months later might be excelling in their basic numerical skills.

One needs to be very careful about putting children into certain categories at an early age on the basis of the screen. I don't think the screen is sufficiently sensitive at this point to really make a diagnosis.

This is an edited version of an interview first published in 2019. To listen to the original podcast, go to bit.ly/Count_Ansari

Tes RESEARCH

Chapter 5
Professor Brett Laursen
Everything you need to know about peer influence

hy are some children so much more easily influenced than others? Can you influence behaviour norms across an entire school? And can teachers be influenced by their pupils? *Tes* spoke with Professor Brett Laursen, professor of psychology at Florida Atlantic University in the US, and editor-in-chief of the *International Journal of Behavioural Development*, to discuss what the research says about the various ways peer influence plays out in schools.

What is peer influence and how does it work?

When we talk about peer influence, we're normally talking about someone getting someone else to change in ways that they might not otherwise do – that can be negative but also positive.

There are two arenas that teachers need to be aware of: peer influence that takes place in the group and peer influence that takes place in the dyad [close relationships].

At the group level, you usually get peer-influence behaviours when you have one person, a leader or someone more popular, and many people in the group are following along behind that leader.

Then, within friendships and romantic relationships, there is a whole other kind of influence. This is typically more private and involves behaviours but also attitudes and beliefs.

At what age does this start to occur in children?

Peer influence seems to peak around the ages of 13-15. There are some cultural differences, but that is generally the case. This is when adolescents start moving out into the world on their own without a lot of adult supervision.

They don't have a clear identity yet, so because they're not exactly sure of who they are and what defines them during these early years of adolescence, they look for somebody else to fill in that gap when parents can't help.

We also know that there are some neurological changes taking place that mean the presence of peers overrides logical thinking. For example, you can assess risks logically all by yourself but, when peers are there, that assessment gets overridden by stimulus seeking and we tend to make not such great decisions when peers are around. This extends into even late adolescence.

Gradually, though, the stimulus seeking gets under control, so to speak, and the logical portion of our brain takes over.

Is there a developmental reason for that?

It's brain maturation. I'm not the person to describe the neurological changes that take place, but it's strictly a function of brain maturation and the regions of the brain that mature at different times during puberty.

So it's something we can't override or control – it just happens at that time of life?

Correct. In fact, there have been several Supreme Court cases in the US in which this kind of developmental evidence on biological brain maturation has swayed the opinions of the justices in favour of not holding teens as accountable for their actions as you would adults.

Is it strange, then, that we have timed the switch from relatively small primary schools to large secondary schools when this is happening biologically?

Yes, that is a structural weakness of how school is set up. I don't like the term "perfect storm", but there are several different factors coming together all at once, which mean that, for these 13- to 15-year-olds, the time when you start moving into these bigger school settings, that's when peer influence seems to peak.

It's a challenging time to be a teen under any circumstances, but then you are tossed into these new, unstructured settings where you absolutely have to have a mate – you need to focus on getting along with others and so peer influence becomes a dominant issue.

Research suggests that because of this, you become more similar to your age mates, to your best friends in particular, during these years than you were before this time, and than you are afterwards, in terms of problem behaviours, such as disruption, juvenile delinquency and drinking.

This makes sense – you really need a friend when you're in high school and you can't afford to lose that friend, so one thing peer influence does is smooth over differences that might arise because we're

changing our behaviours to look more like one another.

Why do younger children not have the same urge to fit in?

At, say, 5 and 6, children think the only view that is important is their own and that everyone else's opinion about their shoes, for example, is the same as their own opinions. But by the time you move into the teen years, you realise that some other people are going to have some different views on shoes and hair, and that perspective matters.

And does this change happen gradually or almost overnight, as children mature?

It's very gradual. There's the cognitive development that takes place, but also children learn through experience.

As you move through primary school, for example, you pick up friends and you learn

the need for minimising conflict or else your friend is going to go play with somebody else. You start to recognise the importance of seeing things through your friend's eyes and minimising conflicts, and that "hey, if we're more similar, then that is going to reduce conflict and make me a more rewarding partner".

A lot of this may not be conscious but, through a variety of experiences, we come to learn the need for getting along with these age mates.

If this happens to us all and it is a natural development, why are some young people so much more easily influenced by their peers than others?

First of all, there are a number of different factors that determine peer influence. On the one hand, a friend could have characteristics that make them particularly influential – after all, influence is not just about the person being influenced, it's also about the person doing the influencing.

There are traits that make some people more able to get others to do what they want. They could be attractive, older, intimidating, smarter, more persuasive; they could just be somebody who is a very valuable friend that you don't want to lose.

Conversely, there are some traits that make people more susceptible to being influenced as well. Obvious ones are children who are younger than their mates, and children who might be more easily intimidated or anxious.

One thing that my research suggests is that if you take a couple of friends, then the one who has fewer options for other friends will be more susceptible to peer influence.

If, for example, you and I are mates and you've got four other friends and I've only

GETTY

got you, or you and one other friend, then keeping you happy is a very big priority for me and I'm likely to do whatever you want.

But you've got six other friends so you don't care about keeping me happy so much, so it's much more likely I will change to resemble you, than the other way around.

This sounds like where the idea of a 'bad influence' might first start arising.

I always caution parents to be very careful in trying to manipulate friendships around the idea that "this friend will be better for them and this friend would be worse for them". It's very difficult to know exactly what the dynamics within a friendship are because you don't know how valuable that friendship is, and you don't know what characteristics the other person brings to the table.

It may be that within a friendship you think isn't so great for your child, it is in fact your child who is influential and bringing along the other child. Whereas if you shift them over to a friendship with someone who you think is more attractive or desirable, then your child may suddenly become the one who is being influenced more and they may be changing to look like the other one, for better or worse.

How fluid – or not – are these roles? Are children generally set in roles of 'influencer' or 'influenced', or can that change?

It's a reasonable question and it cuts to the heart of the question: is being susceptible to influence a trait or is it about the relationships in which you find yourselves and the settings in which you find yourselves?

I would be really hesitant to say, "This person is always going to be at the bottom

of the totem pole and always susceptible to influence under all circumstances". We don't have a genetic marker for being influenced or for being influential.

We've talked about one-to-one peer influence, but how does it play it out in larger groups?

Generally speaking, there are three different kinds of influencers that we see within groups in schools, who use different strategies and tactics to maintain influence.

One is what we would call prosocially skilled individuals, and these are people who are "rewarding partners": they're popular because they're fun to be around, they're probably attractive and probably do well in school.

There's another group of popular individuals who use relational aggression and physical aggression to maintain popularity. These individuals were represented clearly in the film *Mean Girls*,

GETTY

where the popular girls sustained their popularity by using manipulation and aggression to keep everyone else in line.

Then there's the third group, termed in psychology as bistrategic. They use aggression when they need to and then they turn around and use these prosocial things to be nice to people that they were just aggressive towards.

These bistrategic folks are essentially capable of switching between two strategies in a very conscious way in order to maintain popularity, not by fear alone – just enough fear to remind people that that's an option – but mostly then turning around and saying, "Well, I'm really a nice person after all".

Peer influence can often be framed in negative terms, but are there benefits from it, too?

If we go back to the original definition of peer influence – that it's to get people to change and do things they wouldn't ordinarily do – then, yes, that absolutely could be positive, and I would argue that it's just as positive as it is negative.

Positive peer influence gets us to do all kinds of things in life – to do your homework, go home instead of getting in trouble at the bar, to comb your hair, to tuck your shirt in.

Peer influence is absolutely beneficial and is essential for positive social norms. I'm glad you raised the point because it's important for everyone to recognise that peers are at least as good as they are bad in terms of an influence. I would argue that, on the whole, peers are a net plus.

How can teachers, if at all, harness the more positive aspects of peer influences?

It's very delicate because peer influence

has a subtext underneath something we call "group norms". By group norms, we essentially mean what is acceptable behaviour in this group.

If you go from one group to the next, often literally from one classroom to the next classroom, the norms of behaviour are different. It might be easy to get people to do positive things when the group norms are fairly benign and where there's frowning upon misbehaviour. It's very difficult to get peer influence to work in a positive direction if the group norms are "we don't do our school work" and "let's pick on the weak child".

So, first you have to understand the norms of behaviour for the group itself, if you're going to try to nudge the group one way or another.

Can teachers and schools influence these norms of behaviour, then? Is that possible at a whole-school level?

It's definitely worth trying as a way to get smaller groups to buy in to a larger group identity, and absolutely it's not something you would say would have no effect whatsoever. But the crucial point is that it has to then be translated into the small classroom group-level setting.

So, while it starts at the top, it has to be carried down and implemented at each of the subgroup levels. That's the level at which teachers can help make a difference.

However, it's important to note that in any classroom, all the pupils have a shared history together that they are bringing along with them to that room and teachers have to deal with this [regardless of the wider school culture]. As a consequence, the teacher's ability to change the norms of the group is not going to be as easy as one would hope.

What about the other way around – can the pupils influence the teacher?

Oh, sure. There are going to be many parents who had the aspiration of feeding their children vegetables for dinner every night and it has gone by the wayside because, essentially, they were "influenced" to stop aiming for this ideal.

Similarly, teachers can get beaten down in terms of trying to maintain standards and keep the eye on the prize. So, yes, definitely groups can change the behaviours and attitudes of teachers.

But I would argue that this is healthy, in a way. You don't want to have absolutely unrealistic goals that you can't implement. Mid-course corrections are the sign of a competent teacher, I would argue.

Given how important peer influence is to young people, could schools do more to help children with this?

If we're going to continue to persist with school structures that toss children into these large, unsupervised group settings, then we just have to recognise that the most adaptive solution for children is to stick together to navigate these unstructured settings – it's inevitable.

There are some school districts I know that have moved to a structure where they try to keep the classrooms and the children together in smaller groups, so there's not so much time spent during early teenage years trying to navigate these huge structures. But I'm a realist – I know

this isn't going to change tomorrow for most schools.

Can we teach children anything about peer influence, then, to help them understand it more?

The only thing I would say is that, if parents and teachers are worried about negative peer influence, the best course of action is to build positive identity in the child so he or she has a central core to help them make the right decisions.

Feeling good about yourself and knowing who you are and where you're going helps you make the right decisions and helps you pick the right friends, who are then going to reinforce making the right decisions.

The hopelessly lost ones, the ones who feel bad about themselves, and the ones who don't know where they're going or what they're doing – those are the ones who are in need of guidance and, if there are no adults around to provide that, then someone else is going to.

This is an edited version of an interview first published in September 2019. To listen to the original podcast, go to bit.ly/Peers_Laursen

GETTY

Chapter 6

Dr Wendy Sims-Schouten

Short on support: why primaries are struggling with mental health

Although understanding of mental health problems in young people, and what to do about them, is growing in secondary schools, primary teachers still lack the training and tools to identify the earliest warning signs of common childhood disorders, according to Dr Wendy Sims-Schouten, associate professor in childhood studies at the University of Portsmouth and head of the mental health in childhood and education research group. She explains why primary teachers need more support.

Why do we usually picture a teenager when we think about mental health issues in schools?

When it comes to mental health issues and mental health problems, we know that children or young people are more likely to be diagnosed in their teenage years, especially around age 14. That's not to say that there are no signs of mental health issues and problems earlier on in life but, generally, when you think about mental health issues like eating disorders or depression, those are most likely to be diagnosed from age 14.

There will be early signs at primary school – and even earlier – that children are suffering from issues around mental health and wellbeing. It is important to

be aware of this. But it's also important to be aware of the fact that children are developing, so you need to be very careful how we take this forward and how we approach health and wellbeing in childhood.

How do we distinguish between a mental health issue and something that is part of the usual development trajectory?

This is tricky. There are scientific symptoms of potential mental health issues, and if we get involved early on through intervention and prevention, we can make sure that certain problems in childhood

GETTY

don't turn into diagnosable mental health issues.

From that perspective, it is very important to get involved early on in life and to be aware of early signs and symptoms of children not doing well. These are issues around mood changes, behavioural issues, certain kinds of fears, anxiety.

But, again, we need to acknowledge that children are developing and we need to look at the pattern. Everybody has an off day occasionally: you go to school, just don't feel great. But we need to look out for the child who seems to have an off day for a long period of time, or whose behaviour has changed, or who, all of a sudden, seems to have fears and is not able to engage well with their peer group.

Do children perhaps also get better at articulating their problems as they get older?

Yes, an older child would be in a better position to articulate and explain "I'm not feeling great", whereas a younger child might be talking about having a stomach ache and not feeling very well.

There are issues around being able to verbalise it, but there are, of course, ways around this. There are now a lot of books that schools can use. I think the Royal College of Psychiatry has produced some really interesting books that are specifically geared towards primary school-age children that teachers can use to open up discussions around emotions and wellbeing.

What is especially powerful with children are stories that use metaphors. So, rather than asking a child "what is going on?" (which is too direct), you could present them with a story of a snail who is not feeling great, and that might be a story around self-esteem, wellbeing; or another story about a little train who is being bullied and doesn't know what to do. A lot of the time, it is the sense of being powerless as well.

Do younger children understand that they are anxious, and that is the cause of the tummy ache, or do they not even understand their own feelings at that age?

They obviously don't feel great within themselves if there are underlying wellbeing issues, but they may not be able to articulate that. This is why we sometimes see children who have behavioural issues. Sometimes there is a tendency to punish the behaviour but, really, you need to look at what causes the behaviour.

It is very important for adults to step back and look at the child and talk to the child. There is this notion of social buffering. Social buffering is when you have conversations with the child to talk about what's going on and how they are, without being too direct. We have to be very careful what language we use. But it is about opening up discussion and providing tools for children to deal with things.

This is important because we know that 15 per cent of children aged four who have parents with a mental health issue develop a mental health issue themselves. So, there is a direct link between the home situation and mental health issues.

What kind of signs might you see at 4 years old?

It's about extremes. If a child is occasionally a bit off and throws a temper and isn't happy, that's part of growing up. But if day in, day out, the child is not functioning, there might be behavioural issues – the child might be withdrawn or not able to play with peers, or not feeling like they're in a position to do their work – that is a pattern which is quite abnormal.

In that case, we also need to look at the individual child because, of course, there are differences between children. Every child is an individual. It is important to get to know the child. How does the child behave normally? And what is different? If nothing is different, maybe some children are just more outgoing than others.

It's not just home situations that can potentially cause issues. When we look at mental health and wellbeing, we tend to look at home and what's going on there, but there is also quite a lot of evidence that bullying can cause a lot of problems for mental health and wellbeing, which can be long-lasting problems.

Children who are bullied as young as age 3 or 4, and then go through primary school being bullied, will potentially have mental health issues by the time they're 11 or 12. You will also see signs and symptoms when they are in primary school.

Is there a distinction between learned behaviour and a mental health issue we can diagnose?

I have an interesting example here. I was teaching one of our courses in early childhood and one of our students was a practitioner who worked in early years and she told me a very interesting story. She had a five-year-old in her class who was quite aggressive. He used to hit other kids. It was getting out of control and she was worried about it, so she arranged to meet with the mother.

She had a chat with the mother and said: "Your son is quite aggressive and is hitting other kids." And mum walked straight up to the child and smacked him. That gives you a sense that sometimes it could, indeed, be learned behaviour.

It is about getting to know the child and their home situation, but also what is happening in school because, sometimes, you see children who are behaving very differently at school compared to at home.

I used to know this girl who was apparently out of control in school, then at home there was nothing going on. She was functioning very well at home: she had good relationships with her siblings, her parents were fine. So, then you could ask yourself: do we need to look at the school situation? And maybe there is a tendency to sanction or punish certain behaviours. We need to look at what causes the behaviour rather than saying, "you are a bad person and we need to make sure you behave properly".

If you were in a violent home, could you not only be learning the violent behaviour but also end up developing a mental health issue because of that violent behaviour?

Yes. And that's a really tricky one. If you look at mental health issues which are most commonly diagnosed in younger children, it would either be conduct disorder or anxiety disorder.

Anxiety disorder can be a sign of underlying attachment issues or attachment disorder, which could be associated with mental health problems in parents, disorganised attachment at home, but it could also be linked to issues and problems at school, where the child is worried to go to school because they're just not coping.

Conduct disorder is a child who is showing quite extreme violent behaviour to the point where they are harming animals and being destructive. If you look at the evidence of what could potentially cause conduct disorder, it seems to be a mix of nature and nurture.

That is always a tricky thing with mental health issues: we know there is a big environmental element – what's happening at home, what's happening in your life, what's happening at school. But there is also a biological element.

When a child is showing that kind of behaviour where things are getting out of control, what you need to do is get a Camhs councillor involved. There will be a pastoral worker in school or someone who can refer the child, or at least work with the child in the early stages. But educational psychologists need to be involved as well.

It is really tricky to put a label on a child because a child is always developing. The fact that they may have conduct disorder or behavioural issues early on doesn't mean they can't grow out of it, so we have to be very careful we don't label the child.

How much training do teachers have and how skilled do you have to be to spot the early signs of an issue?

There are a number of changes that are

happening at the moment, mostly in secondary school. For example, you have the "mental health first aid" approach, where one or two teachers in every big secondary school are being trained.

We need this in primary schools as well: specific training in recognising early signs of mental health problems, wellbeing issues or emotional issues. Teachers, especially in primary school, are in a good place to get to know the child because they tend to deal with the same children for a whole year. It is different in secondary school.

In primary school, a teacher will get to know the child. It is important for them to step back when they see the child's behaviour and ask themselves what the cause could be. What is going on with this child? Talk to the parents but also talk to other teachers and be supportive.

The other thing we need to be aware of is that, as I said earlier, every child is unique but children also come through their own unique environments. We have children with different parental situations, children from different ethnic-minority backgrounds and, again, we need to make sure we cater for the needs of different children.

There is, for example, evidence that children from black, Asian and minority-ethnic communities are less likely to be diagnosed. The official data suggests that they are less likely to have mental health issues compared with white British children. But you could argue that this is because some of the signs or symptoms are simply not recognised and not dealt with or engaged with.

We need to do far more to engage with ethnic-minority communities and give them a voice. I think it's incredibly important that we do that.

So, what groups of children are most at risk of developing mental health issues?

The World Health Organization refers to certain groups as "vulnerable groups", not because those children are weaker but because of the situation or environment that they find themselves in. Children who grow up in the care system are more likely to be vulnerable or to be suffering from mental health issues. You also have what we call adverse childhood experiences – if a child has, I think, three or more of those, that is quite a significant factor in potential mental health issues.

Also, children from ethnic-minority backgrounds are more at risk simply because of potential racism and discrimination that's not recognised as such. That can have an enormous impact on children.

But we also have to be careful with our own stigmas. There are children who are perfectly fine, and they might grow up in poverty but they have the most amazing and lovely parents. Then you have children who come from more wealthy families and they have parents who don't really care about the child. So, you have a child who might have low self-esteem or has parents who are too permissive and anxious and don't really care either way.

It is about the individual child and acknowledging the fact that children grow up in their own way. Obviously, environmental influence plays a big role but we need to make sure that we are aware of the needs of every child.

When it comes to singling out a child as having a potential

mental health issue, should a teacher always err on the side of caution and let the professionals have a look?

Absolutely. I don't think you should ever label a child or use any mental health language, because it's not something teachers are qualified to do. All they can do is notice what the early signs are. It might be better to refer to those as issues around "wellbeing" rather than "mental health", because as soon as you say a child has a mental health issue, you're almost assuming there is a proper diagnosable disorder, and the teacher shouldn't be in a position to do that. Once things escalate, a child needs to be referred to be diagnosed, if that is needed.

If there has been suspicion or early signs of a mental health problem in primary school, should that information be passed on as part of the transition to secondary school?

I think this needs to be done in discussion and collaboration with parents and maybe even the child.

In some situations, it may not be a good idea to pass on issues that were present at primary school because the child may need a clean start. In other situations, it may be incredibly good for a child to get the extra support and for people to at least be aware of the fact that there may have been some issues around wellbeing, or problems at home, and this may have implications for how the child will do at secondary school.

I think it is very important to also include the parents here, and to take it from there.

This is an edited version of an interview first published in July 2018. To listen to the original podcast, go to bit.ly/SimsMentalHealth

Chapter 7

Professor Samantha Johnson
Do teachers need to know if a pupil was born preterm?

We know much more than we once did about the potential impact of preterm birth on a child's education. Samantha Johnson, professor in the department of health sciences at the University of Leicester, explains how children born prematurely may be missing out on vital support owing to schools' lack of knowledge about the challenges they might face.

What do we mean by 'preterm'?
A full-term pregnancy lasts about 40 weeks. Preterm babies are classified as those born before 37 weeks of gestation. In the UK, that's about 8 per cent of all births. Most preterm babies will be born just a few weeks early, at 32-36 weeks. We refer to those as "late" or "moderately" preterm. There is a smaller group of babies born "very preterm", before 32 weeks of gestation. This makes up only 1-2 per cent of all births. Among those, there is a subgroup born "extremely preterm", before 28 weeks. Being born this early can have significant impacts later on in life.

Has the preterm birth survival rate increased?
We know the overall rates of preterm births are increasing. That may be largely due to increases in the proportions of babies born late or moderately preterm. But at the same time, the overall survival rates for babies born extremely preterm – at 22-23 weeks – are increasing, which means that there are more of these babies entering society year on year.

Is there a common post-birth pathway for these children?
All babies born very preterm will be admitted to a neonatal intensive care unit where they'll have medical care in the first weeks, or maybe months, of life. Those babies born the earliest (less than 30 weeks' gestation) might then be followed up until they are around 2 years of age.

In 2017, the National Institute for Health and Care Excellence produced the first national guidelines recommending what should happen to these babies in terms of follow-up.

What is the potential impact on a child's development of being born preterm?
Every child is different, preterm or not, and every child will have their own strengths and weaknesses. The information that we have about outcomes for babies born preterm is based on cohort studies or groups of children, and often group averages. It is important to note that within

those, there will be some children who have very different outcomes. But that's not to say we haven't begun to notice a particular pattern.

It's important to note, though, that prematurity is a risk factor, rather than a diagnosis, for difficulties later in life. Not every child born preterm will have difficulties.

We do know that the earlier a child is born, the greater the risk for those difficulties. But you may have some babies born at 23 weeks of gestation who go on to have no long-term difficulties and some born just a few weeks early who do.

What sort of difficulties are they likely to experience?

We're starting to see a clear pattern of potential difficulties that these children might have: the "preterm phenotype".

On average, we would say that children born preterm are at risk of cognitive difficulties in childhood, so having low scores on IQ tests, for example. Specific cognitive deficits are also associated with preterm births: in particular, having poor working memory, eye-hand coordination difficulties, slow processing speed and deficits in executive function.

Children born preterm are also at increased risk for attention difficulties, social and emotional difficulties (problems interacting with peers) and also internalising difficulties (such as anxiety). Often, the children may have a number of difficulties that co-occur.

Interestingly, we tend not to see an increased risk of these children having externalising behavioural problems (conduct problems, or being defiant or antisocial).

If you think about how it might appear in the classroom, they may be the children who are quite withdrawn, not finding it easy to make friends, struggling to focus – but they don't tend to be the children who are disruptive or aggressive. For that reason, perhaps these children may not come to the teacher's attention as having difficulties or needing support in the way other children with special educational needs might.

How likely is it that these difficulties will be picked up before a child starts school?

We know from many studies that if you carry out developmental assessments of children at age 2, there's already a significant difference in those born very preterm and children born at term.

Certainly, at least by entry to school, there's some interesting evidence from the Millennium Cohort Study by Professor Maria Quigley and her colleagues, who studied attainment at the early years foundation stage related to gestation and age at birth. Already, the earlier a baby is born, you can see that, on average, they are more likely to have poor outcomes at EYFS across all of the areas assessed compared with children born at full term.

Do you think it is important for teachers to know if a child was born preterm?

[This] is quite a tricky issue, and feelings can differ widely between families. Some of them, maybe half, would prefer the school to know, so they know what to look out for. And there are some who really don't want the school to know – perhaps the child is doing absolutely fine and there are no difficulties evident, and they just don't want that birth history to be drawn to the attention of the school.

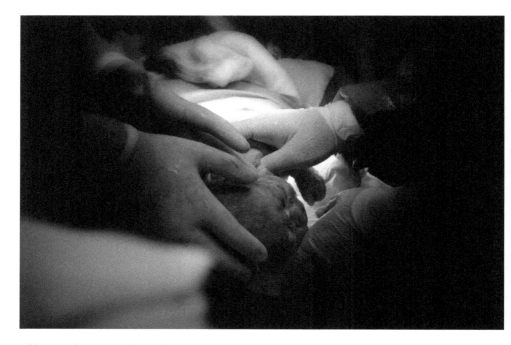

Up until now, the information about preterm births hasn't been routinely communicated to education professionals. Once we start to communicate that and teachers have a better idea of what being born preterm might mean, it may become particularly useful to tell teachers about a child's birth history on entry to school, so they may know what to look out for or can just be aware of it.

How much do teachers already know about the difficulties children born preterm are likely to face and the strategies they can use to support them?

We carried out a survey in 2015 of 585 teachers and about 200 education psychologists in the UK. We asked them to fill in a questionnaire called the "preterm birth knowledge scale". This contains 33 statements about what the likely outcomes are for preterm babies when they reach school age. Those being surveyed have to say for each of these statements whether they are "true", "false" or "don't know". Then they get an overall score, ranging from 0 to 33.

Overall, we found that the teachers had an average score of 15, and educational psychologists had a slightly higher average score of 17.

If you compare that with neonatal physicians, who routinely look after these children as babies, their score was up at 26. So, there's a really big difference.

Interestingly, we found that the poorest areas of knowledge related to teachers' understanding of the risks for children born preterm of having poor social skills, attention problems and mathematics difficulties, which are among the most common difficulties we see after preterm birth. There was concern that perhaps children might not be getting the support in the areas where they need it the most.

We asked teachers whether they felt they'd had sufficient training about preterm birth and only 16 per cent said they'd received any training about it. More than 90 per cent felt that they wanted more information, which has led us to develop a resource to try to improve teachers' knowledge.

Two to three children in an average class of 30 will have been born preterm. We also know that the vast majority of these children will go to mainstream school.

Even among the most extremely preterm babies, a national study, known as EPICure, found that only 13 per cent will attend special schools.

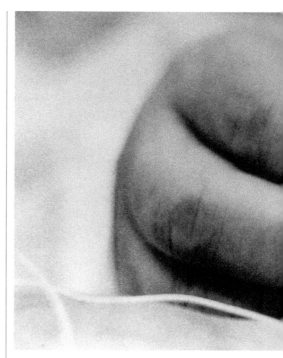

What's happening to children who aren't identified to a school as being born preterm? Are they ending up on SEND registers with different diagnoses?

Among these children, there's a small proportion who have difficulties that are potentially severe enough to have a diagnosis. There's a higher proportion of children born very preterm who will have ADHD or a diagnosis of autism than children born at term, but they are a small proportion of the preterm population.

There are many more of them who could have subtle difficulties in a number of areas that can have quite a significant impact on learning and performance. So, yes, a small proportion will have diagnoses, but I guess there are many more who have difficulties that wouldn't reach a diagnostic threshold.

We do know that there's an increased rate of special educational needs and disability (SEND) among children who were born preterm. The earlier the gestational age at which a baby is born, the higher the prevalence of SEND.

So, the differences can be so subtle that a teacher may not realise anything is proving particularly difficult for that child, when in fact they are not reaching their potential?

That's the difficulty at the moment. If teachers are not aware of the kinds of difficulties that children born preterm might have, those children may not be picked up as having difficulties. They could have attainment within the average range for their age, but their potential could be more with a little extra support. I think raising awareness of the issues that may be associated with being born preterm could potentially be beneficial.

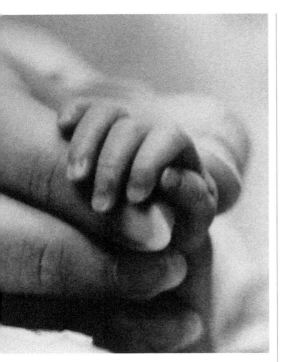
GETTY

give them some strategies and maybe a toolkit that they can use with these children if they are having difficulties.

Hopefully children with significant or severe difficulties will already be identified through the usual educational pathways. Potentially, it is for the children who don't have a diagnosis, and don't have significant problems, that a bit of extra support in the classroom might really have an impact.

And you have developed a resource that hopefully is going to have a big impact in this area?

That's the aim. The survey highlighted to us the need to get this information out to teachers so they are adequately equipped to do their job and support these children.

We found from our survey that most teachers would like more information, but expressed a preference for online resources. So we developed an e-learning resource for education professionals about preterm birth, which represents about one hour of learning and consists of five different learning objectives (bit.ly/JohnsonResource).

It focuses on providing information based on evidence from current scientific literature about what preterm birth is and what educational outcomes are like for children born preterm. There's a particular focus on mathematical skills, as that is an area that these children are likely to have the greatest difficulties with. We also presented information about cognitive and motor development after preterm birth, and about social and emotional difficulties that may be associated with preterm birth.

Crucially, there's a section at the end that provides strategies teachers can use to support children who have the difficulties that are often associated with preterm births. We tried to make it as interactive as

Would it be useful, then, to label children born preterm in the same way that we label those who receive free school meals?

I might not go so far as to say that all preterm children should have additional support because within that group, some children will have absolutely no difficulties.

It's more about raising awareness among education professionals that these children might have difficulties and then they can use their knowledge and expertise to provide support where it's needed.

I do think we have to be mindful not to create the impression, as we mentioned earlier, that prematurity is a diagnosis. It's just a risk factor for problems later in life.

What we want to do by giving teachers the knowledge is to help them signpost where the difficulties might be and then possible, so it's full of audio files, video files, animations, case studies and quizzes to check learning.

We co-designed this with a group of 26 stakeholders, including parents of children who were born preterm, some young adults who themselves were born extremely preterm, teachers, teaching assistants, Sendcos and educational psychologists. So, at the heart of it are teachers telling us what they wanted to know.

It will be made freely available online: we don't want any barriers to people being able to access and use the information.

Has the resource been tested?

Yes. Before we release the resource, we wanted to evaluate it to find out whether it does actually improve teachers' knowledge of prematurity, which is an essential first step in improving children's outcomes.

We were fortunate enough that we have 61 teachers from about eight primary schools who took part in the study. We asked them to fill out the preterm birth knowledge scale that I mentioned earlier and then complete a questionnaire before using the resource and again after using it.

We wanted to see if using the toolkit over a period of up to 30 days would improve their knowledge of preterm birth. We found a considerable difference in knowledge levels before and after using it: beforehand, the average score was 13 out of 33; afterwards it was 28. So, there was a huge increase in teachers' understanding of the subject.

The areas where we saw the biggest increase in knowledge were in recognising that preterm birth might be related to an increased risk for maths difficulties later in life, having poor social skills and having attention problems – the three areas that our previous national survey had shown

teachers were really not aware of. That was particularly important.

We also showed that the toolkit increased teachers' confidence in supporting children born preterm. Before using the resource, just 8 per cent of the teachers felt they were adequately equipped to support the learning of children born preterm. Afterwards, it was 89 per cent – a huge increase. Again, before they used the resource, 23 per cent said they felt confident in supporting children born preterm and that rose to 93 per cent afterwards.

We've shown that the resource does improve knowledge of prematurity and outcomes, and also improves teachers' confidence in supporting these children in the classroom.

If a teacher has just learned that a child was born preterm, should they be concerned, or is it more about incorporating that knowledge into their broader view of the child?

I think it's about incorporating it into the broader view of the child, for the very reason that we don't know exactly what the outcome will be for a child who is born preterm. It is one factor to take into account when we are looking at the individual child and it could be a very useful and important piece of information if a child is struggling or maybe not achieving their potential.

It can signpost where the difficulties might be and give teachers that starting point of where to look. We already know that every child has different strengths and needs, and so it's about just raising prematurity as a potential factor to consider.

This is an edited version of an interview first published in June 2019. To listen to the original podcast, go to bit.ly/Preterm_education

Lightning Source UK Ltd.
Milton Keynes UK
UKHW050644230222
399109UK00006B/133

9 781999 372323